FIND RABID READERS

HOW TO IDENTIFY YOUR TARGET MARKET

CELIA KYLE

READ. WRITE. HUSTLE.

INTRODUCTION

Knowing your target market, how and *where* to find them, and how to appeal to them are "must haves" when trying to write books your readers will crave. You want to write the types of books that touch their hearts, make then think, and get them to act... and those books can't be written without knowing who you're creating for and *why*.

Crafting books that sell requires knowing not only your niche but also your audience and competition. If you want to write books that sell well, start with defining your reader audience.

In this book, you'll learn how to research your competitors, define your audience, how to find them online, and how to best learn everything about them. Then you can truly write the books they desire, not the books you *think* they want. This book will give you the tools to begin your target market research journey, but is in no means a comprehensive guide. You'll be given a good starting point, but as I explain further in the book, this is only the start of your journey into audience research. It absolutely will be an ongoing trek through the reader landscape.

Getting to know your audience in a personal way means you'll be more likely to write books that appeal to them on their level. You'll become part of the community and earn their trust in a way that many authors can't—or won't. They know that you'll always write books they love, and you'll become the go-to author in your niche.

Ready to figure out how to become that go-to author? Then let's get to work!

(*groan* I know, working on this won't be your favorite thing ever, but it's necessary. Pull on your grown-up underwear and hop to it!)

CHAPTER 1

COMPETITOR RESEARCH

THERE ARE a ton of things you have to focus on when you begin to grow your author empire and want to become profitable. One area many authors often forget is researching their competitors. It's one thing to say, "I write like Author XYZ," and another to really understand Author XYZ's business. Yes, knowing about other authors is a small part of your day-to-day life, but it can make a significant difference in the effectiveness of your marketing. In reality, I want you to make sure that competitor research is a part of your author empire and marketing decisions from day one.

Do you know what other authors in your genre are up to lately? You should! Here's why:

What Sets You Apart. If you don't know what your

competitors are doing, there's no way for you to make yourself unique and stand out from the crowd. That means you might offer the same type of book to the same people, in the same way. Talk about #awkward. Being a carbon copy of someone else isn't a good tactic for any business, and especially not something an author wants to experience. You need to give readers what they want in a unique way that no one else is using.

Avoid Doing What's Been Done. What if you have an amazing idea for an ad, but your competitor is already running one like it? Just by knowing what other authors are doing is a great way to make sure you don't waste time and money on something that's been done. Those head desk moments can be avoided! You might even discover that what they've done didn't even work (One less thing for you to waste time on). Let *them* throw money at the advertising wall while you learn and improve on strategies.

Know Your Strengths and Weaknesses. You may have a natural sense of your strengths and weaknesses, but you never *truly* know until you compare yourself to others. Only then can you understand the place you occupy in the market. Comparing yourself to other authors helps you understand how to maximize your natural strengths as well as where there might be room for improvement.

Identify Opportunities. Knowing who your competition is (and isn't) helps you find the gaps where they're not meeting reader wants. Those gaps are your perfect opportunity to fill them. Is there a segment of the reader market that your competitors ignore? You can dominate that segment!

Steal Ideas. Okay, maybe steal is the wrong word. More like, "borrow and modify ideas" or "learn from your competitors' mistakes" are even better. You can keep an eye on other authors and take note of their successes and failures. Analyze these for anything you can learn to help you with your own author empire. For example, if another popular author's book totally bombs, you can figure out why and make sure you don't repeat what they've done. You can improve upon it! If they run an ad for a short period of time before turning it off, it's probably an indicator that the ad or ad site didn't pay off.

Just like "No man is an island," no business is an island. You need to know what other authors are doing so you know what's going on in the market. This will help you spot new trends, new developments in booklandia, any changing tastes, etc.

In this eBook, you'll learn more than simply how to monitor your competition. You'll learn a process for gathering as much information as you can, analyzing the data, then comparing it to your own author business so you can make changes.

The steps are:

Gather Competitor Data → Analyze Data → Assess Standing

- **Gather competitor data.** I'll help you identify your competitors, determine what information you need to gather, and how to get it together.
- **Analyze data.** Here you'll take all of the information you've gathered and analyze it in terms of strengths and weaknesses.
- **Assess standing.** You'll look at the results of your analysis and see where there are opportunities you can exploit. Compare yourself to your competition.

> *Do it to Dominate*
>
> *What do you already know about your competitors, their audience, and how you compare to them?*
>
> *What's your unique niche in the market?*

Gather + Analyze Data

Unlike McDonald's (who probably has a Burger King right down the street), finding your competitors isn't super easy. Sure, you might have a basic idea of who your competitors are, but that's not the whole picture. And we *need* a complete picture for you to be successful. (I want you all to be successful!)

Our first step is to figure out who your competitors are and gather *as much information as you can* for each writer. Start with authors that offer the same or similar books as you right now. These are the guys you're likely to be in direct competition with because readers will choose between buying a book from you or them (we want them to pick you).

Now, I also want you to include newbie authors who will soon offer the same or similar books as you in the future. If you're part of a Facebook group that includes unpublished (or very new) authors who talk about their upcoming releases, make a note of them. It's important to keep your eyes out and plan ahead for authors who will soon be in direct competition with you.

You might not agree, but I feel like your competitors aren't just authors that sell books similar to yours. For example, you might publish your books only in electronic format, but I believe you're still somewhat in competition with the print market. Especially if there's a new release coming from an author with a huge, hungry audience. You need to identify any authors that might cut into your reader base, period.

Locating and Identifying Your Competitors

I want you to start with good old Google. Perform a Google search with the keywords that relate to your genre(s). You can use your main genre, pen name, or type of writing (fiction vs non-fiction).

You can get leads on potential competitors by asking others. Ask some of your contacts and friends which authors' books they buy (other than yours). You can also ask your readers which other authors they know who are similar to you.

Social media is another awesome research tool for hunting up competitors. You can do keyword searches on social media just like you did with Google. You can also peek at your readers' and connections' profiles to see what other authors they like and interact with.

One of your biggest tools is going to be retailer bestseller lists. Every retailer has these, though some are more detailed than others. Meaning, there are some that are broken down by category (fiction vs non-fiction) while others delve deeper and have separate lists for major genres like romance. Even further, sites like Amazon have lists for different sub-genres of romance (i.e. Fiction > Romance > Paranormal Romance > Vampire Romance).

Be careful when perusing these lists, though. Some authors might publish a book that is clearly a paranormal romance but categorize it as contemporary since it takes place in today's world.

Making note of that author as a "competitor" would be a mistake in that instance. You can use the bestseller lists to find authors who write books that will compete with yours, but make sure their books *are* direct competitors first.

Learning about Your Competitors

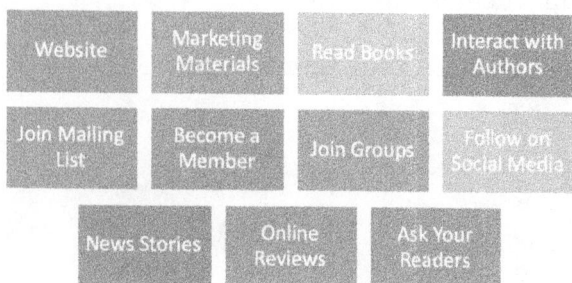

Now that you know who your competitors are, you'll need to gather information about them. A good place to start is their own website. Assuming they keep it up to date (and *you* must), you'll find a ton of information about what they offer, their general tone and approach to marketing, how they position themselves, etc. You should not only check their website but also gather whatever marketing materials you can.

Do they offer swag to readers? Request a swag pack. Is their swag electronic/images? Download those bad boys. Maybe they give away a free book for signing up to their newsletter. Sign up and download the book.

The easiest (and best) way to learn about your competition is to become their customer. Buy their books and *read* them. Sign up for every offer or promotion they have available. For example, if you register for a freebie and you're immediately presented with an email or web page that pushes you to buy one of their books, make a note. This kind of information is good to know. You might be able to gain an advantage by easing up on the immediate sales talk. *Or* you might discover that you're missing out on an awesomesauce income booster that would benefit your readers.

Being a competitor's customer means you should interact with the other author at least once to see how they relate with readers. Contact them with a question (or praise) and see how they respond. Try to think of a specific question about one of their books you've read or ask a question about one of the other books they've published.

Try to have as many points of contact with the author as possible. That means joining their mailing list, becoming a member of their site, joining whatever groups they offer, etc. If the author is going to be at a local conference, stop by their table and have a chat. Directly interacting with them will give you a great idea of what they're all about.

One of the best (and easiest) points of contact is social media. Follow them on all of their social media accounts and see how they interact with readers. For example, if a reader has a comment or question, how quickly do they respond? Do they respond *at all*? Do they respond in a way that you would have? If not, why? What makes them different?

Beyond the author themselves, there are a few other ways to learn about your competitors. Look at anything written about the author by third parties. What does that mean? Check out their reviews. Go to their most recently released books at different retailers (and Goodreads and Bookbub) and see what their readers are saying. What do they love? What do they hate (There's always gonna be haters)?

You can also ask your own readers. Ask their opinions on specific authors; why they chose you over them, or who they go to when they need their book fix. Try to get your readers to be specific. Get them to share specific books (or experiences) from your competitors.

What You Need to Know About Your Competitors

There's no way that you can ever know too much about your competition. Nearly anything you learn can be a valuable asset. That said, here are a few specific things to start you on your research path:

- What types of books (genre, niche) have they published? How are they different from your books?
- Where are your competitor's books available for purchase? (Amazon only? Kindle Unlimited? All retailers? Which?)
- How do your competitors interact with readers? How do they market their books?
- What are your competitor's price points? (All

books at $0.99? Is it a range? How do their price ranges work?)

- What different formats does your competition offer? (Print, eBook, audiobook, translations, etc.) How are those formats delivered? (Retailer print programs? Audible? Draft2Digital? Direct?)
- What does your competitor do to boost reader loyalty?
- What are your competitor's values?
- What is your competitor's brand concept?
- Does your competitor innovate? How (Maybe they have their own app or explore a brand-new social media site)?
- Does your competitor employ any staff?
- Is your competitor involved in any organizations? Charities? Author organizations?
- How do they advertise their books? Online only, or offline as well?

Do it to Dominate

I want you to identify at least three of your main competitors and create a profile for each of them. It should contain the important information outlined in this chapter. You can create the profiles in a Word document or use a spreadsheet to summarize information for each competitor. This way you can easily compare them. Be sure to add other fields you find interesting as you do your research.

You've gathered all of this information about your competition and their customers and now it's time to analyze it all. You'll be focusing on the strengths and weaknesses of your competition. In this chapter, you'll learn several different analysis techniques that you might find useful. It's a good idea to try them all at least once and see which gives you the best results.

Creating a Competitor's Profile

For each competitor, I want you to create a detailed profile. Take all the information you've collected and then organize and summarize it. This will give you an "at a glance" look at your competitor's strengths, weaknesses, market position, and other qualities.

Your competitor's profile should have as much as this information as possible:

Business Summary.
- What they do

Objectives and Vision
- Goal or company vision

Key Competitive Advantage
- What makes them unique

Product or Service Profile
- Features
- Price
- Where sold
- Sales volume
- Target reader
- Other

General Marketing
- How they market their books

Online Marketing
- Various marketing factors

Business Summary. A business summary quickly sketches out what your competitor does. What is their main business? I want you to include the length of time they've been around and publishing. For example, you might have found a British author who has been publishing in the paranormal genre for fifteen years, but recently expanded to science fiction.

Objectives and Vision. Your business includes hard facts, but this area is more psychological. It describes your competitor's goal or vision. This includes their brand image. For example, a paranormal author that only writes about curvy heroines. They might be curvy themselves and offer books proving that curvy ladies can find happiness.

Key Competitive Advantage. Try to find one thing

that makes your competitor unique in the market. This is the author's unique value proposition. It explains how the author meets reader needs in a way that's different from others.

Book Profiles. You might decide to make a profile for your competitors' bestselling book or series. These quickie profiles should include things like genre, niche, trope, price or price range, where and how the book(s) are sold, ranks, etc.

General Marketing. This profile will include information on how they generally market their books. I want you to include external factors like the number of authors in the market (other competitors), trends in the market, and market size. Include percentage of market share and what kinds of marketing they already do.

Online Marketing. You should include online marketing factors like website traffic, website rank, on-page SEO, SEO keywords, and SEO strategy in terms of backlinking and social media activity. Admittedly, this information isn't easy to obtain, but you can use a tool like Alexa to get a good idea. You can also get some broad data by seeing how many social media followers they have or doing a Google search for their books and see where they appear in the search results.

SWOT Analysis and PEST Analysis

There are tons of tools you can use to analyze your competitors. We already use these methods to assess our own businesses, but you can make educated guesses about your competitors without the internal data about their operations.

SWOT analysis helps you identify **S**trengths, **W**eaknesses, **O**pportunities, and **T**hreats. You create a four-section graph and each section represents one of these areas. Then, you simply list the characteristics in each section.

Strengths and weakness are factors that apply to the internal aspects of an author's business. You've already considered these for your competitor, right? During your SWOT analysis, list the main strengths and weaknesses you discovered.

Strengths include:

1. Experience
2. Expertise
3. Resources
4. Relationships
5. Technological skills
6. Brand recognition
7. Frequency of sales
8. Market reach
9. Grassroots (reader) support
10. High level of innovation

Weaknesses include:

1. High cost of operation
2. Weak brand
3. Absence of important skills
4. Low customer retention
5. Lacking customer service
6. Unreliable or low-quality products

7. Missed marketing opportunities (for example, not using Facebook)

Looking at the list of weaknesses above (and this is by no means a complete list), you can easily see how useful this information can be to you. These are places for you to move right on in.

The other factors we'll address—opportunities and threats—are external to your competition. These are things in the market, society, or the world in general. Opportunities and threats are future possibilities. Opportunities are things a company can take advantage of for gain (like gain over your competitors). Threats are risks that could cost an author their position in the market.

Opportunities include:

1. Innovation
2. New technologies
3. Changing customer tastes
4. Favorable change in demographics (for example, aging population, more population in urban environments, etc.)
5. New online distribution channels
6. New partnership opportunities
7. Economic improvements that lead to more consumer spending

Threats include:

1. Unfavorable government policies such as a tax hike
2. Economic downturn that leads to less consumer spending
3. Changing customer base
4. Societal changes that lead to a specific genre or niche falling out of favor
5. Technological innovation that drives price down
6. Decrease of demand for a specific genre or niche
7. Technological problems

PEST analysis is similar to SWOT but takes it a step further. It takes a deeper look at outside factors beyond just opportunities and threats. PEST stands for Political, Economic, Social, and Technological factors.

Political. This includes government regulation, legal considerations, and anything else that might involve the government.

Economic. Economic factors include the exchange rate, interest rate, employment environment, etc.

Social. This deals with changing demographics or trends that occur in society.

Technological. This focuses on new innovations, R&D activity, obsolescence, etc.

Unlike SWOT analysis, PEST looks *only* at external factors. It doesn't even bother with looking at the internal aspect of your competitors' business, period. This is one of the reasons it makes a good partner to the SWOT analysis.

Online Reputation

One last category to include is your competitors' online reputation. Use your social media, alerts, review sites, and contact with readers to create a quickie profile of your competition from the public's point of view. This should be about your competitors' reader's opinion.

> *Do it to Dominate*
>
> *Take some time to create a business profile, SWOT analysis, PEST analysis, and reputation analysis for at least one of your competitors.*

Assess Your Competitive Standing

You know all about your competitor and their place

in the market. Now it's time to compare all of the data to *you* (eep). I want you to make a wholly objective analysis (no lying to yourself) using the previous techniques. It's really, really, super-duper important to be as honest as possible with yourself. List every factor completely.

Ask yourself:

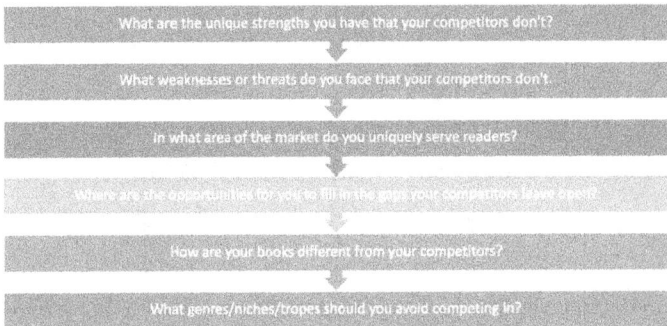

What are the unique strengths you have that your competitors don't?

What weaknesses or threats do you face that your competitors don't.

In what area of the market do you uniquely serve readers?

Where are the opportunities for you to fill in the gaps your competitors leave open?

How are your books different from your competitors?

What genres/niches/tropes should you avoid competing in?

1. What are the unique strengths you have that your competitors don't? In what areas do you already excel beyond your competitors?
2. What weaknesses do you face that your competitors don't? How can you strengthen these weaknesses?
3. In what area of the market do you uniquely serve the needs of your readers? Where are you already meeting the needs of your readers in areas your competitors aren't?
4. Where are the opportunities for you to fill in the gaps your competitors leave open? Look for areas where competitors aren't meeting reader needs but where you can.
5. How is your author business fundamentally different from your competitors in terms of its basic functioning, books, vision, objectives, etc.? How can you play to these differences to set yourself apart from others?
6. What areas should you avoid competing in? These might be areas where your competitor is simply too strong, and you feel you won't have a chance.

Whenever you can, use statistics to get an accurate picture. Compare your sales figures and ranks, market share, social media engagement, web analytics, and any other measurable data you can imagine with your competitors.

Once you finish your analysis, take a moment to review your answers. You should see some trends and spy obvious areas where you can stand out.

If you don't see any opportunities, do a bit more digging. You may have to get a bit more creative (easy, for authors) and get the help of others to figure out how you'll compete. Many people find it helpful to hire an author coach to help them through the process and get an objective opinion. Friends don't count unless you are one hundred percent sure of their objectivity. No one wants to give a loved friend bad news, right? So, unless they can give you the truth with nothing held back, you'll need someone else to give you the nitty-gritty.

Do it to Dominate

Go through everything you've collected and the competitive profiles you created and ask yourself the questions listed in this section.

Pick out one to three areas where you see the biggest opportunity to stand out from your competition and explain why.

CHAPTER 2

YOUR TARGET MARKET

I'VE TALKED about researching your competitors and now it's time to chat about getting to know their (and ultimately your own) readers. This is where you'll learn the down-and-dirty information you need to position yourself in the market.

No matter what you publish, you'll have readers you want to target. These are readers who want your books and the goal of marketing is to connect with those people. Without a clearly defined reader market, you're just throwing things at the wall and hoping they stick without any sense of direction. You have no idea if you're aiming in the right direction!

What is a Target Market?

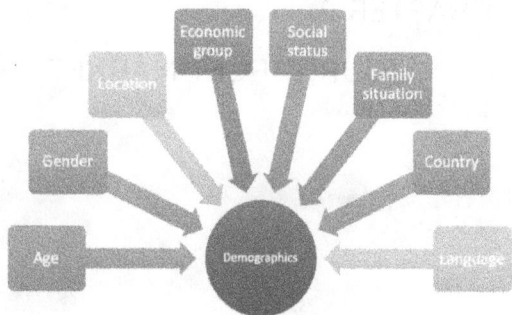

A target market is a group of people who have similar characteristics (and desires) to whom you direct your marketing efforts. It's a very *specific* group of people. You'll define a target market by age, gender, location, economic group, social status, family situation, country, and language. A few random examples might be:

- A resort that targets retirees.
- A clothing store who targets teens who see themselves as trendy.
- A blog that targets (dum, dum, dum) readers!

You'll see that not all of the information I listed is technically "demographic." One target includes teens who see themselves as "trendy."

These type of factors are psychographic data. Basically, how your readers see themselves or the world around them. Psychographic data is just as important as demographic information. A few other examples of psychographic data are:

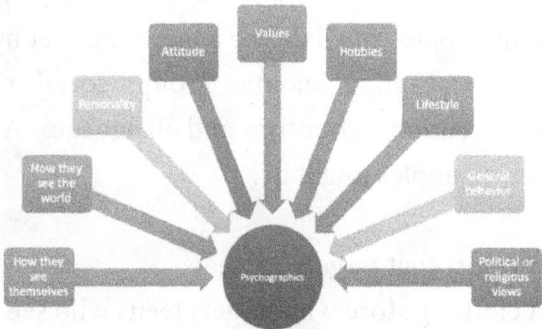

- Personality
- Attitude
- Values
- Hobbies
- Lifestyle
- General behavior
- Political or religious views

Why Laser Target Your Market?

When it comes to marketing, there's no "in between." You either hit or miss. Not targeting your market perfectly means you're wasting your advertising dollars by shouting at the wrong readers. Look at one of the examples I listed above. An ad for your readers would be ineffective if it was shown to people only interested in TV or movies. (*gasp* The horror!) You want readers who—you guessed it —read.

You can't make everyone happy, so your target market needs to be specific. Cast your net too wide and you're speaking to people who have zero interest in your books. They'll tune you out like white noise.

Benefits and Solutions

One of the keys to successful marketing is to identify your market's pain or problem and offer a solution. For non-fiction writers, these seem pretty straightforward. When I created *Read. Write. Hustle.* my market's pain or problem was to help authors with their author business. Seems straightforward, right? Not so much for fiction authors. Your reader's pain or purpose isn't as obvious but boils down to your readers' desire for books in ABC genre, DEF niche, with GHI trope. If you know who your readers are, you can communicate your book's benefits to them in words they understand.

Another benefit is that your readers can relate to each other. By identifying your target readers and marketing to them, you can create a "tribe" that is rabid around these common interests. This is especially powerful online—where readers spend a ton of time on social media, forums, and blogs.

One thing I want you to be careful of when you define your target market is making assumptions. (When you assume you make an ass out of you and me, man.) Marketing is a science (blech) and you need to look for objective data. Research your readers and they'll tell you exactly what they like, think, and want from you.

Do it to Dominate

Write a description of your target market's demographic and psychographic data without doing any additional research.

CHAPTER 3

THE ESSENTIALS OF RESEARCH

MARKET RESEARCH GIVES you a clear picture of your readers so you can write books and grow your author empire by meeting your readers' desires. You must know your market perfectly so you can point them to the books they're craving. In order to do this, you need to gather and analyze hard data about your readers. Remember, there's no point in shouting about your book to the *wrong* readers.

Quantitative vs. Qualitative Data

There are two types of data when you're defining your reader market—quantitative and qualitative. Both types are essential when creating a picture of your ideal reader.

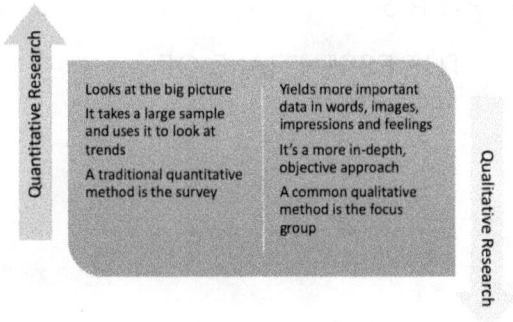

Quantitative Research

Looks at the big picture

It takes a large sample and uses it to look at trends

A traditional quantitative method is the survey

Yields more important data in words, images, impressions and feelings

It's a more in-depth, objective approach

A common qualitative method is the focus group

Qualitative Research

Quantitative is big picture stuff. You take a large sample (over one hundred people) and use that sample to look at trends. If you pick a hundred random readers in your market, you can assume (though I hate that word) that they represent the general reader population.

A traditional way to perform quantitative research is with a survey. With a survey, you might discover that seventy percent of the sample loves your new book cover. You'd then assume that seventy percent of all readers would agree.

Qualitative data is a tricky trickster, but it gives you important data you wouldn't get through quantitative methods. This data isn't based on numbers, but in words, images, impressions, and feelings. It's an in-depth, objective approach where you interact with your sample of readers.

One of the most common qualitative methods is a focus group. You gather a small group of five to ten readers from your reader base and nudge them into a discussion about your books using a set of predetermined questions. You can also include interviews as a qualitative method.

Your Reader Profile

The ultimate goal of your market research is to

create a profile of an imaginary person that represents your perfect reader. This profile needs to be as complete as possible. You should include not only demographic and geographic information, but also how they feel about different things (the psychographic data I mentioned earlier). This is just as important as all that demographic stuff. Psychographic data is made up of things like how readers see themselves, what they're afraid of, what they hope for, and so on. Some authors even give this imaginary person a name. (Mine is Belia.)

A neat trick about having this profile is you can write your sales copy (blurbs and landing page content) aimed directly at that reader as if you were speaking to them face to face.

What You Don't Know

Reader research is a process of discovery. You need to be totally objective and let the data talk to you, not the other way around. The most horribad mistake is to make assumptions. Go into the research process openly and assume you know absolutely nothing about your audience. Rely on *data*, not guesswork.

> *Do it to Dominate*
>
> *Look at the target reader description you just wrote and list the information you're missing. Include everything you'll need to research to create a complete reader profile.*

CHAPTER 4

THREE GRAPHIC SEGMENTS THAT MAKE UP YOUR TARGET READERS

YOUR READER AUDIENCE is a targeted group who has unique characteristics that make them who they are. Those characteristics are things that—in many cases—can be quantified. The ability to measure and track them make it much easier to market to those readers.

Let's start by looking at demographics since that's probably the segment you're most familiar with.

Demographic

Demographics are statistical data about your reader audience. It helps you figure out who is buying your books. This data helps you narrow down who you're going to market to. Here are a few examples of demographics:

- The age of your audience. For example, ages 25-45.
- The gender of your audience. For example, women.
- The income of your audience. For example, an annual income of $50,000 to $60,000.
- Their education. For example, they've achieved an associate's degree or higher.

Demographic data is usually information you can find on a census, is measurable, quantifiable, and tells you who is buying your books. It's much more helpful to know that you're marketing to women ages 35–45 that have a bachelor's degree. Or to men ages 18–45 that don't. The tactics you use and the books you publish are different for those two groups. Demographics play an important role in understanding your audience.

Geographic

Geographic data tells you where your readers are located when they buy. This is significant when it comes to marketing your works. For example, you might have written a small-town novel set in the southern United States. You might want to target only those readers in that geographic area. Did you set a book in Chicago? You might want to run an ad that targets those readers specifically.

Even cities in the same state have different personalities. Dallas, Texas has a different population than Austin, Texas. In addition to ideologies, they have different lifestyles and demographics. It's helpful to know where the target audience resides.

The content you market in these different geographic regions can vary. Think about the varying cultures and holidays in different countries around the world. You need to know where your readers live so you can create unique marketing content for them. A Thanksgiving holiday promotion for a Canadian audience would be different than one in the United States—both in terms of the message you relay and timing.

Once you know geographic locations, you can add power to your marketing and increase your return on investment through segmentation. Both demographic and geographic information can help you take your marketing to a whole new level, *but* it's not everything. You also need to look at psychographics.

Psychographic

Psychographic information is *why* your readers buy your books and is comprised of many variables. Some of these variables are difficult to pin down. I want to look at how to use the information we gather, how to track and measure it, and how to incorporate that into your marketing plans.

Let's first take a peek at some of the variables of psychographics. Psychographics are the traits that make your audience unique and include things like:

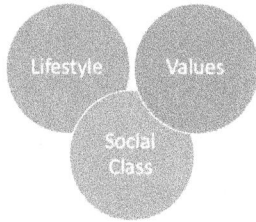

Lifestyle. Where is your audience in terms of life? How do they live it? Are they struggling or highly successful? Do they enjoy nature? Music? Fine arts?

Values. What do your readers value? Are they motivated by their family? Does increasing their income drive them? Are they liberal? Conservative?

Social Class. What's your audience's status and social class? A young adult may struggle financially but be in a higher social class because of their upbringing and college education.

Other elements might include opinions, purchasing practices, personality, and interests. Yes, it can be difficult to gain this information about your audience. That said, once you have it, it can be very powerful. You'll be able to craft marketing messages that speak to your audience, have a stronger conversion rate, and a higher return on investment.

CHAPTER 5

PSYCHOGRAPHIC DATA - BECAUSE DEMOGRAPHIC AND GEOGRAPHIC DATA AREN'T ENOUGH

YOU PUT a ton of time and effort into crafting your marketing strategy and plan. Each part is crafted to get the best results. Your reader audience is defined in your marketing strategy. That research, information, and description is what you base all of your marketing tactics on.

But if you're only using demographic and geographic information, you're missing out on profits and might even be marketing to the wrong people. You've wasted time, money, and effort.

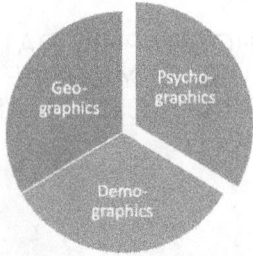

Geo-graphics

Psycho-graphics

Demo-graphics

Take a second and think about this...

The year someone was born—and where—won't tell you if they're likely to buy your books. It's just not enough information. It's a great start, but it isn't enough.

Let's take a look at a writer who's also a business coach. They might attract solopreneurs and small business owners, right? Both of those groups have their own unique needs and goals. Marketing tactics need to be created for each of those audiences. I want to pretend we already know the demographic and geographic information about them.

So, we know that the audience is ages 25–40 who live in the Midwest and central United States and most of them have at least a two-year college education.

That's a great start! You plan on creating content for ladies who are business owners in this age bracket and geographic region. But what if they're made up of conservative single moms? How has that changed the picture? What if these women are high achievers? They're not struggling, are goal-oriented, and attracted to stable brands.

This is going to change the way you market to them.

It gives you more info to brand, build relationships, market, and change how you offer your books.

You realize that geographic and demographic data are just the tip of the iceberg, right? They're part of the bigger picture, but only a small part. You're missing out on the bulk of your data if you don't include psychographic information in your market research and when defining your reader audience.

I also want you to realize that consumers have changed. The abundance of choices and vast amount of information available to consumers has changed the way they shop. A basic example is how we buy coffee today.

Ten to twenty years ago, if you wanted a cup of coffee, you ordered a cup of coffee. Your server might have asked if you wanted cream and sugar, but that's about it. Today? You order a cup of coffee and it seems like you have hundreds of possibilities. The coffee buyer can create and order a coffee drink that fits their needs, mood, and budget.

This coffee example can apply to just about anything nowadays. People research their purchases and look for solutions that meet their unique needs. It's those needs that can change from moment to moment since the world changes a lot quicker than ever.

How people shop has changed, which means that the more info you have about your readers, the better your marketing efforts. The biggest question now is, how do you gather this information about your audience? This process is called "Psychographic Profiling."

The Key Elements of Psychographic Profiling

The first step to having a better understanding of your audience is to create a profile of your reader. You probably already know many of the demographic and geographic facts about your audience. Now it's time to compile the psychographics. This means grabbing three different elements. I want to take a quick look at these, and then I'll talk about the individual pieces.

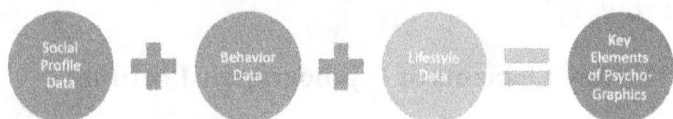

Social Profile Data

Social profile data is—predictably—going to come from social networks. It's made up of the fields that social media users grant permission for the sites to use on their behalf. For example, when you register for a social network, you fill out fields like your relationship status, alma mater, interests, professional affiliations, and occupation. This data often helps you define your audience's social class.

This data is used to create a closer relationship with your reader. Gathering the information is the first step and there are tools that make this step easier.

Full Contact lets you query by Twitter username, Facebook ID, or other contact info to gather social media profile information. Keep in mind that social profile data is only beneficial if it's actionable and combined with other data you find.

Behavior Data

Behavioral data lets you track how your readers behave over time. It separates your readers into groups based on their book reading habits, attitudes toward you, and how they respond to you as a business.

Behavioral data is different from data collected

about a person for marketing purposes. Generally, some types of behavior data include:

- Data collected on ad networks (for example, how people respond to ads)
- Data collected on your website
- Comments and activity on social media sites

Behavioral data focuses on readiness, usage, and loyalty. It's used to personalize your content and marketing. The goal when using this data is to identify and clarify your market's interest and to know where they are in your sales funnel. This info is used to segment and personalize offers, blog and site content, and email messages.

Lifestyle Data

Lifestyle data is the gathering of information about a reader's values, beliefs, interests, and opinions. There are different models people follow and unfortunately there isn't one industry standard. The bottom line is to remember that the info you gather and how you organize it must work with your other data so that it's information you can take action on.

Within these key elements are individual pieces that need to be examined and defined for your audience.

Ten Components of Psychographics

Psychographics are essential to understanding your target market, but what you may not realize is why each piece of information is important. Let's take a quick look at how psychographics reflect your reader audience's living and purchasing behavior and why those pieces are important.

Psychographics gather information about your audience's:

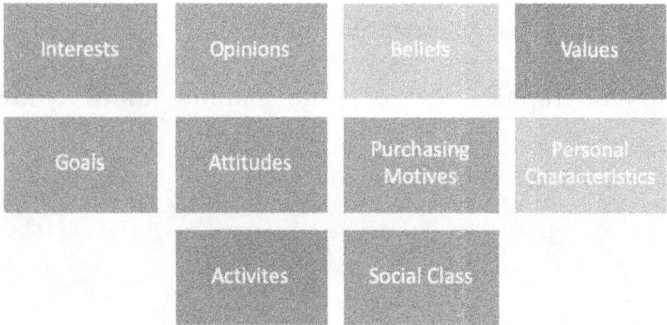

1. **Interests.** What are your readers interested in? Pets, politics, entertainment or technology news? Your readers' interests help you craft the right marketing message. For example, if your readers are interested in politics, using a headline about entertainment news or gossip isn't going to work for them.

2. **Opinions.** Your audience's opinions can spread and change quickly. It's important for you to understand and manage your audience's opinion about you so you can create an appropriate marketing response.

3. **Beliefs.** What do they believe? I'm not talking about religious beliefs here, but what do they believe about success, money, happiness, and other parts of life? You can connect with their shared beliefs or challenge them to get them to open their minds to new ideas.

4. **Values.** These are broad preferences concerning the courses of actions they take. Is their sense of right and wrong important to them? Do they value family over success? Fame or fortune? Connect with your readers' values to engage with them.

5. **Goals.** What do they want to achieve? Are

they bargain hunters looking for the best price, or are they more into brand recognition? If you understand your readers' goals, you can create a message that speaks to them.

6. **Attitudes.** Their attitudes play an important part when creating content. It's a positive or negative evaluation of people, events, activities, or ideas. It also evaluates *you*.

7. **Purchasing motives.** Why do readers buy your books? What's their motive? Do they want to save money? Avoid pain? Feel comforted and connected?

8. **Personal characteristics.** Personality is difficult to nail down but plays a role in creating your reader profile. Is your audience complacent or determined? Are they inquisitive? Demanding? This will help you give readers the information they need to make a buying decision.

9. **Activities.** What do your readers do? What are their hobbies (Other than reading)? What are their traveling and working habits? How do they spend their weekdays and evenings? This can help you create personal messages as well as determine the timing of your marketing efforts.

10. **Social class.** Where do your readers fall on

the socioeconomic scale? Are they professionals? The language you use can be promoted differently depending on the social class you're appealing to.

Do it to Dominate

Write down what you know about your readers for each of the psychographics in this chapter.

Where are you missing information about your readers?

Don't worry about writing a whole lot. This information can be tightened and cleaned up later on, after you've taken further steps.

CHAPTER 6

TOP METHODS OF READER RESEARCH

FOR MARKETERS, the interwebs are a blessing. There's never been so much information about readers at your fingertips. In the past, businesses had to totally rely on costly research methods like focus groups, physical surveys, and other time-intensive data-gathering methods. Online research gives you some quick and effective shortcuts.

Every time you begin a marketing campaign, you need to first gather relevant keywords. Unfortunately, they don't get you much hard data about your target reader other than telling you what they're searching for online.

Here are the top five other methods used to do market research on the web.

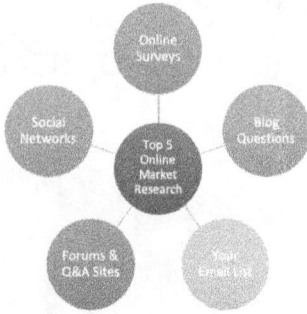

Online Surveys

Surveys have always been a great way to conduct quantitative research and find general trends. In today's age, online surveys are convenient and easy to toss out there into the reader world. You can use sites like Survey Monkey to easily craft surveys that are tallied, and the results presented in an easy-to-read format. Another bonus (to readers) is that they can submit their thoughts anonymously.

Blog Questions

If you run a blog, you can get some super valuable information by simply asking your readers questions. Write a post and end it with a question like, "What do you think about XYZ?" People love to share their thoughts and will eagerly submit a comment. A neat thing about blog questions is that they're versatile. You can introduce a new book or series and ask they what readers think about the blurb, excerpt, or cover image. Ask them their thoughts and feelings when they read/view your newest book's details.

Your Email List

Your email list is the perfect audience for your questions. Mix in questions when you email them about your books or offers from other authors. Ask them questions and use that information for future sales and books. The awesome thing about your list is that they're prescreened. You know they want to be there and are already fans so there's no hunting for someone to answer your questions. It's a built-in audience that are interested in you.

Forums and Q&A Sites

Online forums and question and answer sites are natural places to gather information. Sometimes you don't even need to ask because someone else has already started a discussion on the topic. Curious about how readers feel about the newest Facebook changes? Chances are that people are already discussing the new features.

Social Networks

Social networks are *priceless*. There is so much more happening on there than personal discussions. On sites like Facebook, readers are telling you exactly what they like when they share and comment on the posts they're into. Places like Twitter and Facebook also offer apps to help you with reader research.

Do it to Dominate

For each of the methods I listed above, I want you to note the type of information you want to get from each one.

CHAPTER 7

HOW TO USE SURVEYS AND EMAIL TO UNDERSTAND YOUR READERS

YOUR RESEARCH DATA quality is only as good as your sample readers and the questions you ask them. Ask the wrong questions of the wrong people, and your efforts will be utterly pointless and your time will be wasted. If you conduct your survey in the right way, you'll gain valuable information about how your readers think and shop.

Stick to One Issue

I want you to create a survey with a goal in the front of your mind. Don't try to tackle *everything* at once. Decide what specific, targeted information you want to know. This will help you keep the survey focused. It's better to do multiple surveys for different types of information then to overwhelm people so they leave the survey incomplete.

If you want to ask people about what genre they read, stick to that topic. If you want to discuss their frustrations or problems when they're shopping, make that the focus.

What to Ask

Having a clear goal makes figuring out what questions to ask super easy. The best strategy when coming up with questions is to simply make a huge list and then go back and eliminate the ones that don't really apply or overlap too much with others.

All questions should be easy to answer and not too open-ended. Don't challenge or frustrate your readers. Otherwise they'll give up on the survey and leave you without any data. Don't ask them something like "Would you buy this book ten years from now?" Personally, I have no idea if I'll buy a book tomorrow, who knows what I'll be doing in ten years!

Avoid leading questions. You want objective data about your readers' thoughts. Don't lead them to agree with you. Leading questions will just taint your results and the answers will be useless. Avoid questions like, "Do you feel like $0.99 books are driving down prices and are obviously super crappy so a book priced at $4.99 must be insanely better?"

Remove any questions that aren't relevant. Every question should be in line with your goal and give you information and data you can use. You're taking people's valuable time when they answer your survey.

Some examples of questions might be:

What are the biggest challenges you face in your life or work?

Why are those challenges a problem for you?

How have those challenges affected your life or work?

What do you do now to deal with those challenges?

Why did you choose those solutions?

How well do those solutions solve your problems?

- What are the biggest challenges you face in your life or work?
- Why are those challenges a problem for you?
- How have those challenges affected your life or work?
- What do you do now to deal with those challenges?
- Why did you choose those solutions?
- How well do those solutions solve your problems?

Lastly, try not to offend or alienate your readers. Everyone has different thoughts and feelings, so assume your readers are sensitive to controversial subjects. Don't ask them how much money they earn and then ask them to include their names. Don't touch anything political or a hot topic in the news today.

Tools to Make It Easier

There are quite a few software tools you can use to make crafting surveys easier and will give you sample questions to ask. One site is Survey Monkey that will let you create surveys and polls super quickly. The site is easy to use, and it's all completed online. There are lots of customization features including things like allowing readers to skip questions. There are also templates you can use if you're not sure what to ask.

A more advanced site is Zoomerang, which has been around for more than ten years and is used by quite a few Fortune 500 companies. (Which means it's probably too much for the average author, but a gal's gotta give you all the info.) Everything is customizable and it has a ton of features. Zoomerang is fancier than Survey Monkey, but it also costs a lot more.

Give Them a Nudge

There are lots of people who are happy to give you their opinions, but you can entice readers to participate by giving them an incentive. Give readers something like a small freebie, entrance into a contest, a coupon, or some other type of discount. Offering a freebie is a pretty common method and it's a great way to get fence-sitters to complete your survey.

Who Do You Send Your Survey To?

If you've already got a newsletter list, you can send your survey to those readers. If they already know and love you, they'll generally be happy to give you their opinions and thoughts. But if you don't have a pre-qualified group, there are several other ways of getting your survey out there and in front of reader eyes.

- Go where they are. If you know a good percentage of your readers can be found on Facebook, create Facebook ads that give them something in exchange for taking the survey.
- Link to your survey everywhere. Advertise it in your email signature, blog, or a big link on your site.
- Get a ready-made audience. Some platforms like Survey Monkey have a feature that lets you choose your target demographic and get feedback from that audience.
- Enlist help. Are you on good terms with other authors within your genre? Tap into their audience. Ask them if they'll send your survey to their readers in exchange for sharing the data you gather.

> ## *Do it to Dominate*
>
> *Using the sample questions and your notes about what info you need about your readers, identify the goal of your survey, then draft five to ten short questions readers can answer. Set up a free account*

at Survey Monkey to set up your survey and make it ready to share.

Make a list of places you'll share your survey and how you'll encourage readers to submit their answers.

Surveys aren't the only way to get data. Email is another great way to perform research. It's cheap, easy, and gets your results fast. An email list is a pre-screened group of your target market. By signing up, these readers have expressed an interest in your books. Here are some tips on how to use your list effectively for market research.

Email Makes Surveys Easy

The biggest advantage to sending a survey via email is that it makes it easy for readers to respond. All your subscribers have to do is hit "reply" and the results are sent to you. Make it even easier by giving readers checkboxes to click. They don't even have to enter any text! You can include an opinion form at the bottom if they want to leave comments.

Opinion Surveys by Email

Opinion surveys are excellent and work well through email, but they involve more action on the part of the reader. This can mean response rates aren't as high. That said, the information you receive will be more in-depth and of higher quality. These are surveys where you throw out a suggestion or ask for ideas and readers respond with their opinions. Because you're asking them to do more, it's important to offer an incentive or reward for participating.

The Dreaded Delete Button

The downside to email surveys is that darned delete button. Readers can click the button and make the email disappear forever. There are a couple ways you can reduce the risk of being deleted but it's still gonna happen. One way to lower the chance of deletion is to make sure the "from" line tells the readers who you are. The "subject" should explain exactly what your email is about. Tell readers why you want their opinions and how you're going to use their responses to give them the books they crave. Don't forget to tell them how long the survey will take!

Spicing Up Your Surveys

A fun way to encourage participation and spice up the process is to include images or other attached files. This takes advantage of email's capabilities and makes surveys more engaging and entertaining.

Share the Results

People hate being left hanging so share the results with the readers. You can do this via email or by posting the results on your blog. Let readers know when and where they'll be able to see the results. Don't forget to thank them!

The Disadvantage of Email Surveys

And now to the disadvantage of email surveys—not everyone uses email. This will limit your audience for your survey. If you need input from readers of all ages and demographics, email may not be the best method. Email surveys work best for groups that use it often: business people, college students, association members, or subscribers to your list. Keep this in mind when you plan your survey.

Do it to Dominate

Using the ideas I discussed, create an email to your list that asks them to complete the survey you just created.

Note how you'll share your results.

CHAPTER 8

HOW TO USE PSYCHOGRAPHIC DATA IN YOUR MARKETING

I'M GOING to bet that you've spent the time, energy, and money to gather your psychographic data by now. That means you understand who your readers are, how they behave, and why they behave the way they do. You know their needs, wants, and motivations. Now what? What do you do with the data you've collected?

You use the information to grow your author business. Your marketing strategy is going to be impacted by your customer profile. Your branding and books can speak to your readers' wants and needs.

How you promote your books can reflect the information and data that is important to your readers. Your sales copy, blog posts, email content, headlines, and language you use will include the benefits and language that your readers want and understand.

Your call to action can be tweaked to speak directly to your readers. All parts of your marketing strategy will be impacted by your psychographic data and a greater understanding of your readers.

Ways to Use Your Psychographic Data

I want to take a look at five ways you can use psychographic information in your marketing.

1. Customer Profiles

2. List Segmentation

3. Language

4. Marketing Channels

5. Sales Copy

- **Customer Profiles**

Any time you create a marketing plan you need to keep your readers in mind. You may have originally created a customer profile as part of your business plan and probably only used demographic information along with some guesses about psychographics.

With this additional research, you have more information to work with and you can use your psychographic data to create a very detailed and narrowly focused customer profile.

Take a look at what you've gathered and see if there are ways to divide your readers into distinct profiles. Most importantly, I want you to look for key differences, similarities, and any trends in the needs, personalities, behaviors, and other psychographic data. During the process, you'll also rule out characteristics that *are not* part of your readers' profile, too. Those elements are equally important to keep in mind. For example, your readers might respond better to casual language and be totally turned off by formal or pretentious-sounding words. (Blech!)

- **List Segmentation**

With your new and improved reader profile, you can apply that information to your email list. For example, an email to men might be quite different than an email to women.

While both may be on your list, the marketing messages will be different. Depending on the features of your mailing list software/email platform, you can segment your list to make sure each reader gets the right info from you.

You probably won't be able to use this kind of segmentation right away, and you may decide to move to a mailing list service that has more features. Your current service may not have segmentation like this available to you, meaning they might not be able to gather the data you want and automatically segment your subscribers.

Be sure to take a peek at the abilities of your current list provider to see what they can do. If you're going to check out a new system, make sure it has the ability to segment your readers.

- **Language**

When you create your profiles and marketing content, keep in mind that you might use different language for the different types of advertising. To totally generalize, guys might be more responsive to masculine language and sports metaphors, whereas women might not. Social media abbreviations and trendy talk might appeal to young adults while your over sixty-five crowd may not understand them.

Even something as simple as pronouns can make a difference. If your target readers are primarily women, you'll want to refer to "she/her" when talking about reading your books. It will make it totally relevant to your target reader and make her feel she's included.

When you get to writing your marketing content, keep your reader profiles in mind and base each message on the profile you're using. Look through your data again if you're not sure of the language you should use. More importantly, make yourself a list of dos and don'ts when it comes to the language you use. Make sure anyone who creates content for you has a copy of these standards as well as a copy of your reader profiles.

- **Marketing Channels**

The channels you use for delivering content, communicating your message, and promoting your offer will be different depending on the reader profile you're marketing to.

For example, Pinterest has been described as a great social media site for women while men aren't as likely to use the platform—though that's not a hard and fast rule. Marketing channels like social media change over time, especially as their audience gets older. You don't love the same things today as you loved twenty years ago, right?

Use your psychographic profiles when you're doing your planning, choosing your channels, and developing your tactics. Look for where your readers are hanging out online. See where they're doing their socializing, research, shopping, and buying. Then you can target your messages to where they are *and* what they're doing in those places.

If your target reader is hunting for "how to" books and ideas on Pinterest, create a board for "how tos" that link to your books. Then, if they go to Google to search for something, make sure you have SEO'd the heck out of those pins and your board using the language they use. That practically guarantees they'll find your pins, content, and books.

If another segment of your readers gets recommendations on Facebook, you want to focus your marketing in getting your books in front of that group with a giveaway or contest. Something that's targeted at giving them exactly the kind of books they want will get their attention.

- **Sales Copy**

You absolutely don't have to send every reader to the same sales page. Your promotional content, sales page, and promotional material can all be created for your different reader profiles.

Try setting up a different landing page for the various segments of your market. Depending on who you're marketing to, you might want to use the relevant URL/sales page for that market. You might use different ads with different copy going to a different URL. That could even mean utterly different promotions or list-building giveaways.

Then split test your sales wording for your segments. These are called A/B tests and will tell you what works best for your different customer profiles. You might use two versions of a landing page for your female readers and only change the headline for each. When you publish new content or promotions that send people to different landing pages, you can use Google Analytics to send half your traffic to one version of the landing page versus the other.

When you hyper-target your sales copy, you'll probably see a jump in conversions.

I want you to remember to use your customer profiles when writing any type of content for sales pages, emails, books, contests, promotional items, and prizes. A man might want to win a ticket to a sporting event while a woman might prefer a spa package. Of course, that doesn't mean women don't like sports events, but your reader profile should give you these kinds of details.

> ## Do it to Dominate
>
> *Review your data and write at least one reader profile.*
>
> *Break down your information into more profiles if the data revealed there are differences and groupings within your customers.*
>
> *Ask yourself how these profiles should change what you're doing in your marketing. What are you going to do differently in each aspect of your marketing?*
>
> *Where can you revise your marketing approaches?*

Psychographics will take your marketing strategy to a whole new level. Without this info, it's like trying to have the same conversation with your grandmother as with a teenager. Those people have different goals, experiences, and language. Psychographic data gives you the ability to talk to your readers in a way that they'll respond to.

CHAPTER 9

WHERE TO FIND READER DATA

BY NOW YOU should be following your competition on social media. That's also where you'll learn a lot about their readers. Pay attention to your competitor's biggest fans on social media. These are the readers who interact the most with the author. You should identify those readers and follow *them*, as well. They're probably the most active on social media so there's a lot you can learn from them.

| Follow on Social Media | Join Groups | Sign up for Alerts | Ask Other Author's Readers | Conduct Surveys |

Join the groups your competitor's readers join and participate in. These might be related to your genre and niche or they might only be vaguely related. For example, if you're publishing science fiction books, there might be a paranormal fiction group that many of your competitor's readers also belong to.

Another great way to keep tabs on your competition is to sign up for alerts using your competitor's names. One easy way to do this is with Social Mention. With Social Mention, you register to receive alerts for your chosen keywords. (Author names!) Whenever someone posts something about the author on one of eighty social media sites, you get an email alerting you. You can use your competitor's name or book title with Social Mention and get notified whenever someone mentions them.

Another option is to contact your competitor's readers directly. Conduct an online survey and invite them to participate, offering an incentive (freebie, anyone?) to sweeten the deal and encourage them to respond. A second option is to hold a focus group with your competitors' readers. Be transparent about what you're doing, but don't bill it as a method to gather information on your competitors. If you hold a focus group or do a survey, use it to learn about reader needs. Then you can add questions about other authors they buy from, too.

One quick way to create a survey or learn more about your competitor's readers is to launch a social media ad campaign. This is pretty easy to do if you're already following your competitor (you are, right?) and know their fans. Social media ads allow you to target people based on likes and interests. Yes, this involves some cost, but it's not a lot, *and* it's something you only have to do occasionally in order to reach out to your competition's readers.

Do it to Dominate

Pick at least one of the methods I mentioned in this chapter to learn more about your competitors' readers. Keep track of what you find.

CHAPTER 10

TARGET READER PROFILE

THE WHOLE POINT of research is to gather data to ultimately give you a picture of your target reader. When businesses do this, they create a customer profile. This is their ideal customer—one who wants and needs their product. It's very detailed, in fact the best customer profile will be as specific as possible. Some market researchers even give their ideal customers names, and some even post pictures of real people who represent their market.

Why Reader Profiles Are Important

Knowing your audience is an essential part of being a successful author. You need to know your audience intimately which can be hard if you're trying to attract everyone. Your readers aren't everyone. It's not even everyone involved in the niche you want to target.

Once you've created one reader profile and have perfected your marketing for them, go on to create sub-profiles for the different segments of your audience. For now, I want to focus on the "audience of one."

Why You Want to Reach an Audience of One

There are quite a few reasons why you want to market to an "audience of one" rather than working to appeal to the masses. Mainly, you'll increase your reach and ultimately revenue, but let's take a peek at some of the other reasons.

You'll Get Rid of Freebie Seekers

These are the readers who will download any free book that they can. They're the readers who download your freebies, read your blog, join your groups, and get on your list but never share anything. They never comment or engage and merely take up space. They might be great people, but they cost you time, money, and put your conversion rates in the toilet. Blech!

You'll Save Money Marketing

When you're crystal clear on who your readers are,

then your ads, content, and even your books will be more effective. Everything you do will be laser focused on your "audience of one's" needs and not those of everyone in general.

Your Messages Will Be More Focused

No one wants to get all political, but you ultimately do need to think like a politician and focus only on your audience. Don't stress too much if you offend your non-audience—focus only on your readers. You'll bring your target readers closer to you! Take a minute and watch some political ads on YouTube to see what I mean. You don't need to be as offensive as some of them are, but they're good examples of how to focus only on *your* target.

You'll Save Time

Attempting to please everyone all the time—even if they're on the fringe of your audience—is time-consuming and exhausting. Let's pretend you're trying to market an adventure excursion at a specific resort in Mexico. (Aw, yeah!)

Why would you advertise that resort to anyone who can't afford the trip? Sure, some who come across the ad might be sad they can't afford it, heck they might even be angry. But that's okay, because those who are in your audience will book a trip. If you're wishy-washy about the cost, you might be contacted by those who can't afford the vacay. This wastes your time and theirs.

Your True Avatar Will Share You

The readers who truly enjoy your books—who are likely to be happy when targeted well—will become hard-core referrers for you. Spend the time to get to know the readers, target the right person, and give them what they want at the right price, and it's a no-brainer that they'll support you. They'll be happy to share with everyone they know! Birds of a feather flock together, right? The same concept applies to readers everywhere.

You Can Personalize Better

An "audience of one" is much easier to personalize. You can address sales content to "Boomer Women Who Want to Travel Alone to Mexico" rather than *all* single women who want to travel. This will speak to your audience in a way that will mean so much more to them. You can even share inside jokes because they'll know exactly what you mean.

This isn't going to lower your reach or income. Actually, by laser focusing on an "audience of one," you'll probably reach more people, get more traffic, and make more money. (Which is what we all want, #amiright?)

What is an Avatar?

I'm not talking about the movie "Avatar." I mean the way that you create a vision of your perfect or ideal customer. One of the secrets to connecting with your readers on a deeper level is to bond with them emotionally. To do that, you need to get with them on an individual basis—or in a way that feels as if it's on an individual basis. Picture them in your mind, understand how they think, what keeps them up at night, and the problems they face that only *you* can solve (This last bit pertains to non-fiction authors specifically).

The only way to laser target your readers is to get a clear image in your mind of your ideal reader. One way to do that is to create an avatar—or reader profile—that shows your readers' persona. The avatar will show what they look like, what they do for a living, what scares them, or gives them joy. It'll also reveal what you can do for them.

It all begins with the reader. Who are they? What's their primary fear? What is their deepest desire?

Creating an avatar is very important and useful because:

- You'll be able to send clearer messages.
- Your messages will be laser targeted to one person.
- Creating targeted content will become easier.
- Developing effective ads will be simpler.
- Book creation becomes almost automatic.

The reason you need to create a complete reader profile is so that nothing you do going forward is generic and bland. Your books will be targeted in a way that no one will mistake you for anyone else. Who you're talking to will be clear and unmistakable. If you can get into the mind of your reader—feel what they feel, desire what they desire, need what they need, and fear what they fear—everything you do will perform better. Everything you write will resonate with your ideal reader in a way that's truly effective.

Creating a reader profile helps keep you from generalizing your audience. Your audience isn't all "single moms" or all "work-at-home people" or even "business owners." Your audience needs to be laser targeted and narrowed down to a "market of one."

Let's look at what you'll need to create your perfect reader profile.

Demographic Information

Earlier I pointed out that the basis of your reader profile is demographic information. These will be personal stats and include:

- Age or age range
- Gender
- Geographical location
- Level of education
- Type (or specific) occupation
- General income level
- Family structure

Your customer might be a thirty-something single mother working a professional job who lives in the suburbs of a large city. Or you target male Americans living outside the United States who earn over $80,000 per year.

Lifestyle and Hobbies

Lifestyle and hobbies are another important factor. These are considered psychographic details. Some examples of lifestyle and hobby data are:

Free time activities

Eating and health habits

Smoking and drinking

Clubs and organizations they belong to

Places they frequent

- Free time activities
- Eating and health habits
- Smoking and drinking
- Clubs and organizations they belong to
- Places they frequent

Psychographic data is as important as demographic data, if not more so. You might target well-to-do women in their twenties who rock the nightlife on the weekends. If your books are best enjoyed on the weekends indoors while the reader is curled up on the couch...you're not going to advertise to the weekend partier.

Morals and Values

Psychographic data gets to the very core of how readers see themselves. You'll want to clearly define their attitude and beliefs about themselves, the world around them, current events, and books like yours. In this category would be goals, aspirations, and where they see themselves in the future.

Pain Points

One other important part of psychographic data is your reader's "pain points," or where the market is lacking so you can offer them a solution—your books. Define what frustrates them and what problems they face when shopping. It's good to know what solutions they're hunting for.

Shopping Habits

How does your market shop? This data should address how much they spend, where they like to shop, and how many books they buy on average. As a marketer, it's your job to bridge the gap between books and readers ready to love them. That's why this information is essential.

Stereotyping Can Be a Good Thing

Are you looking at all this and thinking "aren't you stereotyping the market?" Of course I am! But it works. By creating a profile of your ideal reader, you're aiming your marketing efforts at the right people. Otherwise you'll cast your net too wide and your message will be irrelevant. You'll waste your resources and advertising dollars. Create your marketing materials and sales copy by talking to your ideal reader and the right people will hear about your new, awesome book.

> *Do it to Dominate*
>
> *Use the info you collected throughout the eBook to craft your target market profile.*

CHAPTER 11

WHERE DO YOU FIND YOUR READERS?

EVERYONE HAS TOLD you (or they should have) that you need to know your audience so you can create books that appeal to them. Plus, knowing your readers' minds before you even write a book will ensure the book is successful when you publish. It's much easier to offer a book to someone when they already want it than it is to write the book first and find the readers later.

There are a few benefits to knowing your reader audience, like being able to weed out the audience that may only vaguely like your books versus those that will gobble up your books as if they were starving. This is going to allow you to be more effective with your marketing *and* your writing. If you know exactly who you want to attract, you can focus your messaging in a way that makes those readers feel special. A great thing about knowing your audience is the fact that you can avoid wasting your time on readers who have to be heavily convinced to buy your book. You want those readers who are *craving* your work.

In the chapter titled "Target Reader Profile," you developed a clear reader profile after completing your research, right? If you haven't yet (shame on you), here's a quick recap of the info you'll need and the "whys" of defining your audience.

When you define your audience, the most important factors to keep in mind are:

- Age range
- Gender
- Income level
- Location

You can create surveys for readers you think are part of your demographics and use Facebook ads to attract survey takers. You can conduct interviews of your competition's readers and even form focus groups to give you more insight into your audience.

What do they look like? What problems do they find in books they read? What makes them buy a book?

Once you ask some of these questions, it'll be easier to find them so you can observe them in their natural habitat.

After defining your audience, you can figure out the message you want to deliver to them in your marketing. But first, you need to find them! This way you can truly get to know them inside and out as you craft the message you want to deliver using words and tone that they'll identify with.

Find Them Online

Okay, you better have your audience defined by now or so help me... You can now locate where they hang out online. They may be on specific social media platforms, niche sites, forums, or groups.

When you join your readers, you're becoming part of the group so you can develop connections that are going to be deeper than if you inserted yourself below or above them. When you join them as an equal, you can empathize more and write even better books for your readers.

Join Groups. Do Google searches and poke at social media to find your readers and join groups and networks where they interact. Then sit back and observe them before you start participating. Just join three to five online groups at a time to keep yourself from being overwhelmed. As you watch them and determine if your audience is really present, you can then choose to stay or move on.

Stand Back. Avoid the urge to dive in and immediately talk about your books. Instead, I want you to get to know them so you can write books that answer their questions or complaints and fulfill their desires. You can interact with them once you get to know them better.

Be a Resource. Instead of constantly trying to sell, sell, sell to readers, become a resource. When readers ask questions, answer them if you can. If you know of someone else who might be able to help, recommend them. No matter what, you should avoid self-promotion. Let your page or profile speak for itself.

Become an Authority. As you get to know your readers, find ways to show that you know what you're talking about. This applies more to non-fiction authors, but write an eBook, host a webinar, and fill your blog with relevant information. Only hand out stuff your audience wants—and needs—to know about.

Go to Live Events. You've gotten to know your audience online, but how about in real life? Attend live events your audience attends. It's an amazing (and fun) way to get to know your readers.

Update Profiles. I want you to update your profiles on *all* social media you use. This way, when you're being helpful, people can look at your profile. From your profile they can find a link to your website that then offers them a freebie to join your email list. This is a much better approach then constantly trying to sell in groups that aren't yours. When you're impressive, readers will check out your profile.

I want you to wholly integrate yourself into your readers' world. Pay attention to what they say and make any of your responses about *them* and *not* you. Doing this is one way to guarantee your success. The thing is, when you've joined your reader audience, your experiences there only matter when you connect with reader wants, likes, and needs.

CHAPTER 12

BECOME PART OF YOUR READER AUDIENCE AND INTERACT

YOU'VE FOUND your audience and you're ready to interact with them now, right? This is all about building a relationship with readers which will lead to them learning to trust you. When you know what they care about, you'll be able to talk with them on their level and make it even easier for them to trust you.

Popping into a group and immediately screaming your sell, sell, sell attitude won't make a good impression or make you any friends. Really, readers are going to get annoyed and angry at these types of "drive-by" posts without taking two seconds to join a conversation. Seriously, don't do the drive-by thing. It's not pretty. Engaging with readers is the key to truly joining readers so you can get to know them.

You'll make stronger connections if you take the time to immerse yourself with your readers, so you become part of the community.

Plus, you'll totally learn about your ideal customer on a new level. You'll be on the inside and easily find out what your readers want, need, and desire.

Immerse Yourself. Bless your heart, but don't go into a group and post about yourself right away. I want you to watch, listen, and learn. You need to get to know your audience in order to give them what they want.

Make Connections. You'll be meeting people in your niche groups, forums, events, etc. and will make strong connections. Do more than like their page or follow them on Twitter. Find other ways to connect such as tagging them when you post something they might like. (And I don't mean your own book!)

Learn Their Language. While you immerse yourself in reader groups, you'll learn the language they use. When you pay attention to the words they use, it'll be easier to use these phrases in the books you write and your marketing.

Note Their Wants, Needs, and Desires. That phrase again #amiright. While you become part of your audience by being part of groups and forums, I want you to note their wants, needs, and desires. This will help you when you're creating content (like blog posts) and writing books. For example, if a bunch of readers ask the same questions or have the same gripe, this is information you can use when you start your next book.

Read What They Read. Find out the most popular books readers are cracking open. What books are being recommended most? If you do this, you'll be able to put yourself in their shoes and easily understand what they're gobbling up. You can even ask them what their favorite books, magazines, and blogs are to read. (Which, you know, I consider engagement, which is what you should be doing anyway, right?)

Listen to What They Listen To. I don't mean music (Though I always love a good music recommendation). What I mean is, do they follow specific podcasts? Ask the groups what they're listening to. Ask them why they like it. Then take some time to listen to those podcasts and start a discussion about something interesting you heard. You'll show that you care about what they're listening to *and* you'll be engaging.

Getting to know your readers will pay off because you'll build trust with your readers. Build it in a way you couldn't if you didn't take the time to figure out who they are, what they want, what they need, and how you can give them everything they desire.

Being part of your reader market turns you into an insider. *But,* I want you to keep in mind that what you experience is subjective. Even if you're part of the group, what you experience doesn't make it a fact or what a majority of the market experiences. Take the time to study the issues instead of making assumptions. Just because Reader A feels a specific way doesn't mean that *all* the readers are the same.

CHAPTER 13

TRACKING YOUR RESULTS

YOU'RE NOT new to tracking your results, right? (You better not be!) You should already be tracking your click-through-rate, conversions, traffic, and engagement on social media. Something like Google Analytics—free with a Google account—is one tool you can use to track your results. There are also free analytics and insights available on some social media sites included with your account.

What's different now is that you're not looking at all the results in one big batch. You'll look at the results over time within each segment. Thinking back on the man versus woman reader profiles, you wouldn't look at their combined results.

Instead you'd look at the effectiveness of your marketing for the man segment and the woman segment separately. This is going to require an organized system for tracking and measuring results. Google Analytics offers segmentation features to make this easier for you.

In addition to tracking click-through rates for your segments, you'll also keep track of conversions, engagement, buying, and segment retention. You might discover that women make a lot of purchases right away, but then drop off and out of your sales funnel. Men might stay in your sales funnel for a longer period, but purchases might be spaced out and less frequent. This information will help you craft various messages for your segments. You might decide to add more content to help with purchasing decisions or just to keep your readers' attention.

Examples of Measurement Tools

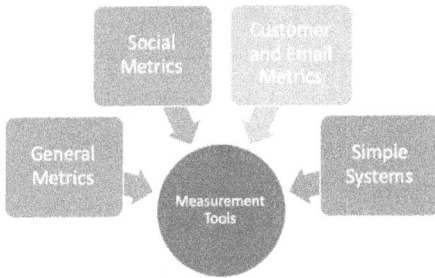

General Metrics. I've mentioned Google Analytics as a tracking and measurement tool that you can use to measure traffic and clicks. You can also use it to track goals and complete sales funnels. If you set it up properly, it'll give you information about social media traffic, your ecommerce site, and all other neat variables. Take a look at the site and pick one or two things to focus on since it can be very overwhelming at first.

Social Metrics. For social media metrics, you can take a look at the data each social media site offers, but there are tools that can give you even better insights. One tool is True Social Metrics. They've got a 30-day free trial and offer segmentation.

Email Metrics. There are a lot of email autoresponder systems that give you list segmentation features and analytics that help you manage when and what kind of information you send to readers.

Simple Systems. You don't just have to leverage a bunch of technology to measure your results. There are some simple systems you can put into place to make sure your different audiences get unique information. You might create a unique URL or promo code for your different audiences. This way, you can ensure your data is pure and only relates to that specific reader segment.

Whenever you create content for your audiences, like separate URLs or codes, track what you created and where it's being promoted. At the most basic level, you can use a spreadsheet to keep track of this part of your marketing. Leave space to record the results of your efforts—such as a conversion rate for each.

As you create your marketing strategy for your segments, this is also the time to decide what you're going to measure and how. What information will you track and how will you track it?

When you look at your results how will you know you're successful? Build these tracking systems into your strategy and make sure you're able to gather the important information so you can continue to strengthen your marketing.

Do it to Dominate

Explore the different tools available to you and decide how you'll track your data.

What tracking will you start doing now? What do you plan to do in the future?

Keep a record of results you discover right away using the information you have on hand, such as from Google Analytics. Don't worry if you can't do this right away. It takes time to gather data on changes in your marketing.

CHAPTER 14

YOUR CHANGING MARKET

JUST BECAUSE YOU'VE done your market research and crafted a customer profile, doesn't mean you're done. Since people and the market are constantly changing, research is an ongoing process. If you don't keep up with the times, your message can quickly become irrelevant. A book that matched your market last month might be overlooked today.

Conduct Regular Market Research

Unfortunately, market research isn't a one-and-done deal. You have to keep on top of it constantly. Whatever methods you used to conduct your research, put them into your regular schedule. Don't just conduct the research when you start working on a new book, publish a book, or have a problem with sales. Make it part of your regular operations even if you have no immediate need for updated data.

Improve Your Offerings

One reason to constantly research is to offer improved books to your audience, often exceeding their expectations. Authors who stay in touch with their readers and ask for feedback discover ways to give readers what they want. You improve your knowledge of reader tastes, likes, needs, and desires every time you head back into the research cave.

Keep in Touch Online

You never want to get out of touch with your target market. You need to keep communication open and freely flowing. The interwebs offer a ton of ways to keep in touch with readers that are cheap, easy, and fast. Ways like:

Social media

Blogging

Online surveys

Feedback forms

Online forums

- **Social Media.** Have a strong social media presence and engage with your fans and followers on a daily basis.
- **Blogging.** Regularly write blog posts and try to get readers to interact and start conversations.
- **Online Surveys.** Conduct surveys and analyze the results regularly.
- **Feedback Forms.** Everywhere you can, give readers a feedback form where they can submit anonymous comments.
- **Online Forums.** Keep on top of what's going on with your readers and in your industry by hanging around forums related to your author business.

Don't Make Assumptions

When authors fail to perform ongoing research, they make one of the costliest assumptions possible. They assume (blech!) that their readers' tastes won't change over time; that their books will always be in demand. On the other side of that coin, authors who keep their eyes and ears open and stay in the loop can change with the times. Never assume and never just "hope" you'll get it right. Base your decisions on hard data collected from your target audience.

" *Do it to Dominate*

From the ideas I listed, note the ones you can put into regular practice to always keep track of your target market.

Make a list of your next tasks and put a deadline next to each.

CHAPTER 15

PUT YOUR READER
KNOWLEDGE TO GOOD USE

BY NOW, you've learned all you can about your competition and your target readers. It's time to put it all to good use. Yay! Take time to write down what you've learned instead of telling yourself that you'll remember everything. You won't, and that means you'll have wasted oodles of time. Seriously, get out a pen and paper (or a Word document) and take notes.

Keeping notes about your competition and audience will make it easier when it comes time to create content (any kind of content) for your audience. You'll create things that will attract, nurture, and motivate readers to want to get to know, trust, and eventually buy from you. (Which is ultimately what we all want.)

Let's take a second to talk about what constitutes content.

Content is any info you create and provide online for your readers. That includes paid advertising, blog posts, videos, images, infographics and... books! If your readers read it, watch it, look at it, and consume it—it's content. (Seems pretty straightforward, right?)

But how do you know what to create for your "audience of one?" You need to create something that informs, engages, entertains, teaches, or inspires your readers to take action.

All of this can be hella challenging because you need to create content that engages your target readers wherever they may be in the buying cycle. This is where your reader profile is important. You can peek at the image you've created, including everything you've filled out, and read through it whenever you create content.

What Stage in the Buying Cycle are They in?

There are several types of buying cycles for the various niches, but the buying cycle begins when the reader realizes that they have a specific problem or need. They do research, compare books, and then make a decision to purchase one of those books. Let's look a little deeper into this. Ready?

Awareness of Problem or Need. Your reader needs to realize they have a problem that can be solved in some way.

Research. Your reader knows they have a problem so they begin researching for solutions… your book!

Comparison. They've found a solution, now they'll compare books to see which they'd like to purchase.

Purchase. They pick YOUR book and purchase!

Retention. Now you've got the opportunity to interact with them through more personal and targeted methods including emails, blog posts, and articles; through videos, webinars, and podcasts; and on sales, landing, and opt-in pages.

By knowing your "audience of one" you'll be able to create the right type of content that informs, engages, entertains, teaches, and inspires your readers to take action on your books and other offers.

Now to talk a bit more about putting your knowledge to good use!

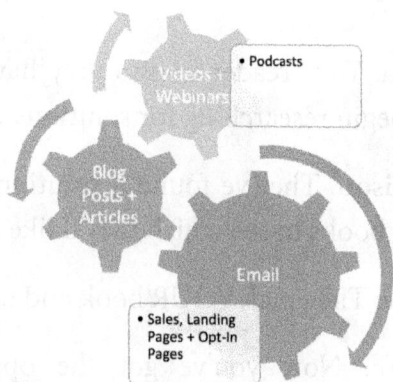

In Email

What you send to readers via email is really important. Some people even say that emails are more important than anything else. You should think of your email list as a group of readers who are in your inner-circle. This will make it easier for you to figure out what you should share with them.

What you send via email will not only help educate readers, but also nurture them so they stay on your list and be more responsive. Every email you send will teach them how important your emails are and how important it is to open each and every one.

Let's look at some of the emails you can send your audience.

- **Welcome Them.** The very first thing a reader should receive when they join your list is a welcome email. Make this one count because it's more likely to be opened than *any other* email you send. I want you to tell them what to expect from being on your list, send a survey that will help segment them better, and take a moment to cross promote your social media networks.
- **Send Resources to Them.** You can send them a resources email which means sending

an email that shares several resources that you like and use. You might send one type of resource per email (which means your email is shorter and you can send more) or include everything you recommend in one email. There's no wrong answer here.

- **Send an Unexpected Freebie.** It's always nice to send your list members something nice for no reason at all. For example, let's say that you see the same question being asked in the groups you've joined. Develop a short report as a freebie and send them the link. This is another awesome way to segment your audience.

- **Get Answers to a Survey.** Want to find out exactly what your audience wants? Send them a survey. In the email, you'll describe your question as well as give them a link to the survey. (Survey Monkey is a great resource here.) Depending on who you use to host your email list, you can set up your email autoresponder to segment your audience based on their answers.

- **Answer a Question You Saw.** If you keep seeing repeat questions on social media and in your groups, you can answer that question in an email to your readers. Use the question as the beginning of the email and answer the question or, even better, answer the question in an eBook or course they can snag.

- **Be a Great Resource by Sending Curated Content.** One thing to keep in mind is that you don't have to create all of the content you send to your readers. You can point out other things that are important and then include your commentary. The best way to do this is to first create a blog post with the content recommendation and then link to your post in an email to your readers.

- **Let Others Brag About You Via Email.** Did you get a new testimonial/review that made you feel awesome? If so, send an email to your readers that announces the testimonial and give a link to it. Always link the product (eBook or course) that prompted the testimonial, too.

- **Monthly Newsletter.** Send out a weekly or monthly newsletter. The best way to compile your newsletter is to include some new content, but you can also point to content you've already included in a past newsletter. Essentially, you'll point out what's new for the period the newsletter covers as well as some other recent happenings. You give a shout out to some of your most hard-core readers and ask your readers questions. (Engage, engage, engage!)

- **Build Buzz in Email**. A fun email that always gets me good engagement is one where I hint about what's coming up. Whether that's a giveaway, some type of promo, or a new book. When you're excited, they'll be excited for you. If you have anything upcoming that's on your mind, even if it's not happening until next year, this is a great reason to send an email.

- **A Day in the Life.** This is a fun type of email that will help strengthen the connection between you and your readers. You can describe your life on any given day. You can make a blurb about it that links to a longer blog post, but it's nice to include exclusive content so your subscribers feel special.

The more often you email your list the better, *but* you also want to remember that you should have something important to say before you click the "send" button. Keep your emails shorter than a blog post and make sure your email links to something that will give them more info, a resource, or something they can buy.

In Blog Posts and Articles

Now that you know more about your audience, you'll be able to create the type of content they desire. Use what you gathered during your research to make compelling blog posts and articles. Keep that in mind as you create different types of blog posts and articles for your readers.

- **Create a How-to Blog Post.** This is an awesome and easy type of blog post to create. You can include images, video, and text depending on how difficult it is to express your concept. Use what you've gathered from connections to help you figure out what they need to know.
- **Develop List Posts.** Lists are very popular. A list post is simply a numbered list about a topic. Let's say a lot of readers in a group have said something like "How Can I _____?" If you know several ways to answer the question or can recommend several resources to do whatever "it" is, write a post for your readers.
- **Craft a Series of Posts on One Topic.** Writing a blog post series on complex topics is a great way to create content for your readers that can be turned into cornerstone content. Cornerstone content is content that reflects your business's goals and missions. A

fun thing about series posts is that you can also turn the compiled posts into a PDF and use that mini-eBook as a way to bribe people onto your email list.

- **Create a Resource List.** If you use (or know about) resources your readers need, this is another great type of post. You can turn it into an article (instead of a blog post) and link to it from your main menu, too. Use affiliate links when you can to add a little bit of income to your pocket.

- **Develop Checklists.** Create checklists, cheat sheets, and to-do lists. These can be a blog post and a download to get readers onto your list.

- **Write Product Reviews.** If you use someone's products or services and you think your readers will like them as well, doing a review is a fantastic way to create useful content. Sometimes you can even earn some pocket change via an affiliate link.

- **Create Infographics if You Have a Lot of Data.** Any time you have statistics or any other type of numerical data it's a great time to create an infographic. They're an effective way to put a picture in your readers' minds for any post or article that includes a lot of data.

- **Post Videos or Podcasts Instead of Text.** Tip: A blog post doesn't have to be text-only. You can also create a vlog. You can record it, post it to YouTube, and then embed it in a blog post. It also doesn't hurt to give readers a transcript for search engine optimization purposes or as a downloadable file.
- **Conduct Interviews.** A fun way to get known in your industry and give readers some great content is to interview industry leaders, happy customers, and anyone else who might have something to say to your audience.
- **Transcribe Audio or Video.** Whenever you have audio or video, take the time to transcribe and post it whether that's on page or in a special report.
- **Accept Guest Blog Posts or Articles.** An easy way to create content with minimal work is to let other people write for you. Set up a quick way for others to submit guest posts or articles for your blog. You can choose what content to accept and give others some guidelines to follow before submission.
- **Write Guest Blog Posts or Articles.** Guesting wherever your audience finds content is an effective way to bring readers

to your website. Find out where they read and submit content to them. You may be surprised to discover that others are happy to publish your post and provide a link back to your site. (Tip: Create a special landing page for the guest post so you can track its effectiveness.)

Using what you learn about your audience as an active participant will help you figure out what they want and need to know. Then you can turn that yummy information into inhalable blogs and articles.

In Videos and Webinars

What you learn from readers can also be used as ideas for videos and webinars. Basically, any time someone asks a question, it can be used as a webinar or quickie video.

- **Product Demonstrations.** A lot of times doing a demo of a product is a lot easier than explaining something with text. You can do these demonstrations either live or pre-recorded and post it at a scheduled time.
- **How-to Tips.** You can create short videos with one tip per video and then post it on YouTube or Facebook (or both) and then

embed the video on your website or blog. The ideas for the tips should come from questions you've gathered from readers. Make sure the tips are relevant!

- **Customer Q&A Videos.** This is a great way to use Facebook Live or YouTube Live. Let readers know when you'll be live and then allow them to ask you questions. You can answer yourself, but if someone else can answer, let them weigh in.

- **Expert Q&A Webinars.** Invite an expert you've been watching (even if they're your competition). They can do an expert Q&A about something important to your readers.

- **Video on a Sales Page.** A fantabulous way to use video is to put it on a sales page. Doing a video to explain why someone needs what you're selling is more authentic and relatable than mere text.

- **Explainer Videos.** You've seen those explainer videos where a difficult to understand concept is explained by a spokesperson and whiteboard, right? These can be fun and explain a point in a memorable way.

- **A Greeting.** You can record a greeting to your readers. Use them on your site, social media, and any other place you can imagine in order to develop trust. Remember to use words and phrases your audience finds comforting.

These are all great ways to use video and webinars to connect with your audience, but you can probably think of even more for your readers. When you take part in groups, keep a notebook of the information they find most important and useful. That information will help you develop the best content for your readers.

In Podcasts

One other type of popular content is podcasts. This is audio that your readers will listen to by using a service like iTunes. They also might go directly to your site and listen to your podcasts there.

Podcast content can be developed from anything you've created for any other platform. You can use the information in your blog posts as a jumping-off point for your podcast. You can use questions your reader audience have asked in groups or forums. You can also take inspiration from other podcasts you've listened to if you think you can cover the topic in a better way.

There *are* some good rules for podcasts that you should keep in mind. Make sure you get your ideas from your readers and not just randomly plucked from your mind without doing research. Next, I want you to ensure your content fits the following criteria.

- **Podcasts Should Be Personal.** When you're talking to your readers, tell them your story (or someone else's) in the most personal way possible. You want to connect to your listeners on an emotional level.
- **Stay Relevant.** Your topic needs to be relevant to your readers. One way to stay relevant is to listen to other people's podcasts in your niche. Look at any comments left, see how many times it was downloaded, and find out what the listeners think about the podcast. Improve on their format and fill in the gaps.
- **Conduct Interviews.** Podcasts are always a "more the merrier" situation. The listener feels like they're getting an insider's view of experts talking about a topic. You can find people to interview by using the information you gathered about your target market and knowing who are considered the experts and gurus.
- **Audience Participation.** Sometimes it's fun to let your readers participate by asking

them to join you during your podcast. Let them interview you and you can interview them.

Podcasting is an awesome way to create new content because once you record the podcast, you can repurpose and reuse it many times. Your readers can enjoy your podcast while exercising, doing housework, or driving to work without having to give it one hundred percent of their attention. (Like they would during a webinar or reading a blog post.)

But it's important that you get ideas from your readers. When you do that, they'll feel like you can read their minds even though they're the ones who told you what they want.

On Sales, Landing Pages, and Opt-In Pages

It's easy to forget that sales and opt-in pages are also places for content. It still needs to appeal to your readers. Truly, it's even more important that you use reader language so they can relate to your offering immediately.

There are a few things every landing page needs to include, but you need to look at it through your audience's eyes. The person who is going to answer the call to action. The best way to figure out what content you should use is to watch them on social media, know who they like to follow, which publications they read, etc.

- **Headlines.** A great headline will talk directly to your readers in a way they'll understand while it also clues them in on what they're about to read when they click through.
- **Persuasive Content.** Since you know your audience well (right?) you can create content that makes them want to know more. You know what's keeping them up at night and how to fix their problems in a way that gives them hope.
- **Tell a Story.** One way to come at a landing page is to tell a story that they want to see unfold. You can tell them a version of their own story that will include grabbing your book (or course), following the steps and ultimately succeeding. You'll only know how to tell this story by watching and learning from them.
- **Explain Why "You".** Every page should show that you're the right person to trust. Use the words they use when talking about their issues.
- **Make it Chunky.** This has nothing to do with your audience, but I want you to make your landing page chunky with sections

broken up with white space. Use subheadings, bullets, and mini-headlines.

- **Elicit Trust.** Your readers should trust you to get them to follow your calls to action. What's the best way to do this? Answer their questions before they even ask. You already know these questions by seeing readers ask them in groups, forums, and other sites.
- **Provide Social Proof.** This will be a lot easier if you're active with your readers online. Give them examples that show how your approach revealed in your book works. When you see others talking about your book on social media, ask them if you can use their story.

Knowing exactly what your readers want should make it super easy to create content that they'll inhale. Make sure you don't just study your audience once. The one-and-done approach isn't going to work. You need to study them continually. Think about how people have changed over the last ten, twenty, thirty years. The demographics may stay constant, but their ideals might change. You should be constantly learning about your ideal audience on social media, forums, and other online hangouts.

FINAL THOUGHTS

IF YOU'VE BEEN FOLLOWING ALONG and handling all the "Do it to Dominate" action steps, then you should have the beginnings of an action plan. If not, no panicking! It's time to sit down and create a strong reader profile for your audiences.

Within your profile you'll include a description of your readers *with* psychographics. I want to put together a plan for gathering and analyzing the data you'll need.

- Gather Demographics & Geographics
- Compile Psychographics
- Create Audience Profiles
- Integrate into Marketing Strategy
- Track Your Success

Go through your current reader profile gathering the demographic and geographic data for those readers. Then pull together the psychographic data for your audience. Think about starting with your email list and social media followers. There are several tools I listed throughout the book, plus there are tons of free and other paid services online.

Create a detailed description of your audience profiles. I want you to keep in mind that you probably have more than one target audience. Once you have your profiles in hand, let's go back to your marketing strategy and integrate your new profiles into your strategy. For example, your plan might include different email subject lines for your different profiles.

Your final step is to make sure you have some sort of tracking process so you can monitor your success. Remember that you don't have to work your reader profiles into every marketing channel/initiative at once. You can totally start small. You might want to apply your psychographic profiles to your email marketing first. This is where you might see the biggest results. You can then add things to your sales copy, advertising, and gradually move onto every channel and phase of your plan.

FINAL Do it to Dominate

Set tasks and deadlines for the following:

Gather demographic, geographic, and psychographic data for your audience

Create reader profiles

Determine marketing tactics

Measure and track results

FREE COMPANION WORKBOOK

WITH SO MUCH data that needs to be compiled in order to properly research your competition and join your readers, I created a printable PDF workbook specifically for writers who purchased the eBook version of this book. To download your printable PDF companion workbook, go to https://readwritehustle.com/go/rabidreaders-workbook/

This file is for writers who have purchased this eBook via retailers or the *Read. Write. Hustle.* website only. Please do not share this link with others.

TARGET MARKET ARTICLES FROM THE BLOG

HTTPS://READWRITEHUSTLE.COM/BLOG

- Welcome and Why It's Important to Speak the Right Language
- Quick Start Tip — Spy on Your Competition
- Speaking Your Market's Language on Social Media
- Using Your New Language Skills on Your Sales Pages
- Testing New Language as You Learn It
- Finding the Right Words to Overcome Objections
- Evolving Your Language as Your Target Market Evolves
- Using the Right Language & Terms for SEO

LIST OF PLACES TO GATHER DATA

Keyword Research

Google Webmaster Tools

Google Trends

Keyword Tool

WordStream

SEO Book

Ahrefs

Keywords Everywhere

Alerts

Social Mention

Mention

Hootsuite

Zoho Social

Awario

Sendible

Buzzbundle

Social Media

Facebook

Twitter

LinkedIn

YouTube

Review Sites

Amazon

Barnes & Noble

Kobo

Apple Books

Goodreads

Bookbub

ABOUT THE AUTHOR

Ex-dance teacher, former accountant and erstwhile collectible doll salesperson, New York Times and USA Today bestselling author Celia Kyle now writes urban fantasy, science fiction, paranormal romances, and non-fiction.

It goes without saying that there's always a happily-ever-after for her characters, even if there are a few road bumps along the way.

Today she lives in Central Florida and writes full-time with the support of her loving husband and two finicky cats.

Find Celia on the web...
www.celiakyle.com
www.readwritehustle.com

www.ingramcontent.com/pod-product-compliance
Lightning Source LLC
Chambersburg PA
CBHW070934030426
42336CB00014BA/2672